Learn About

ANIMAL HOMES

BURROWS

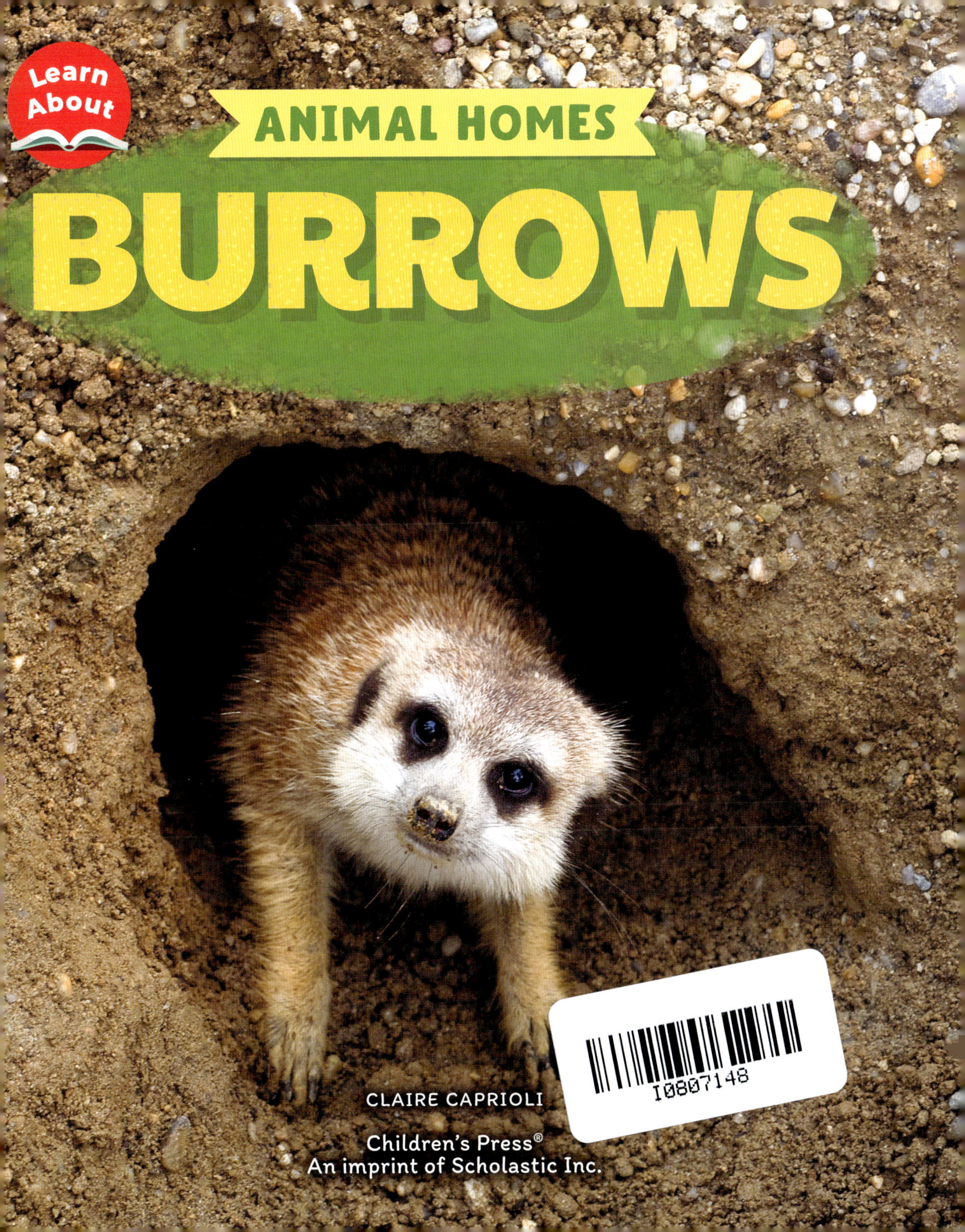

CLAIRE CAPRIOLI

Children's Press®
An imprint of Scholastic Inc.

A special thank-you to the Cincinnati Zoo & Botanical Garden for their expert consultation.

Library of Congress Cataloging-in-Publication Data available

ISBN 978-1-5461-7701-2 (library binding) | ISBN 978-1-5461-7703-6 (paperback)

10 9 8 7 6 5 4 3 2 1 26 27 28 29 30

Printed in China 62

First edition, 2026

Book design by Kay Petronio

Photos ©: cover, 1: dnberty/Getty Images; 2: Marius Roman/Getty Images; 3: GlobalP/Getty Images; 6–7 grass and throughout: SpicyTruffel/Getty Images; 7 main: Martin Harvey/Getty Images; 8–9: Dave Watts/Alamy Images; 10 top: Burt Sytsma/Getty Images; 10 bottom, 11 inset: Marius Roman/Getty Images; 12–13: Andrew Daview/robertharding/Alamy Images; 13 inset: Marius Roman/Getty Images; 14 top: GlobalP/Getty Images; 14 bottom: Carlos Carreno/Getty Images; 15 main: Jose A. Bernat Bacete/Getty Images; 15 inset: GlobalP/Getty Images; 16–17: Dorling Kindersley ltd/Alamy Images; 17 inset: GlobalP/Getty Images; 18 left: Martin Harvey/Getty Images; 20–21: Frauke Scholz/Getty Images; 22 top: VitalisG/Getty Images; 22 bottom: JAH/Getty Images; 23 inset: VitalisG/Getty Images; 23 main: Chris Mattison/Alamy Images; 24–25: Farina Graßmann/imageBROKER/Shutterstock; 25 inset: VitalisG/Getty Images; 29: Tom McHugh/Science Source.

All other photos © Shutterstock.

CONTENTS

INTRODUCTION

NATURE'S BURROWS

Have you ever dug a hole at the beach? Or crawled through a tunnel at a playground? Some animals make their homes out of holes and tunnels! These are called burrows. Burrows keep animals safe and warm. Animals can dig burrows in dirt, sand, snow, or even between rocks. Let's learn about how different animals make and use burrows!

This puffin's burrow keeps it safe.

Chapter 1

WOMBATS

FACT FILE

ANIMAL GROUP: Mammal

DIET: Herbivore

HABITATS: Forests, mountains, and woodlands of Australia

FACT!

Wombats spend most of the day sleeping. They do not like the hot sun. They come out of their burrow at night to find food.

A wombat peeks its head out of the entrance to its burrow.

Wombats are strong! Their bodies are built to dig burrows in dirt. Some wombat burrows have one room. Others have more rooms and extra entrances. Wombats will often make more than one burrow. More burrows mean more places to sleep. And more places to stay warm or cool.

An adult wombat usually lives alone in its burrow. But mothers and babies share a burrow. Wombats are marsupials. That means their babies are carried in a pouch.

This young wombat still shares a burrow with its mother.

FACT!

A baby wombat stays in its mother's pouch for 5 to 10 months. It lives with its mother in the burrow until it is one-and-a-half to two years old.

A mother wombat's pouch opens toward her back legs, not toward her front legs. This way dirt doesn't get in her pouch while she digs. Wombats dig with the claws on their front legs.

Chapter 2

PUFFINS

FACT FILE

ANIMAL GROUP: Bird

DIET: Carnivore

HABITAT: Coastlands

FACT!

Male and female puffins dig a burrow for a baby puffin together.

Puffin parents use the same burrow year after year.

Puffins make their burrows along cliffs by the ocean. They dig their homes in the ground or between rocks. To dig a burrow, they use their bills. They also use their feet to kick the dirt out of the burrow. Their burrows are about 3 feet (1 m) long. That is close to the length of a guitar. It is enough space for a puffin family.

Puffins make burrows to stay safe. And to keep their babies safe. A baby puffin is called a puffling. Only one puffling is born at a time. The puffling stays in a nest with bits of feathers and grass.

FACT!

Both parents take care of the puffling in the burrow. They bring it fish to eat. The same parents will have a new puffling each year.

The nest is at the back of the burrow. There is a bathroom area inside the burrow, too. It is separate from the nest. That helps keep the nest clean.

A puffling is born with a gray beak and gray feet. Both will turn orange as it grows up.

Chapter 3

EUROPEAN RABBITS

FACT FILE

ANIMAL GROUP: Mammal

DIET: Herbivore

HABITATS: Grasslands, woodlands

FACT!

The European rabbit thumps its back leg to warn other rabbits. This means to go back to the burrow for safety.

This rabbit uses its front legs to dig burrows. Its back legs kick away the dirt.

European rabbits dig special burrows in dirt. They are called warrens. Warrens have many tunnels and rooms. They can hold hundreds of rabbits. The warrens also have many entrances. This allows the rabbits to hide easily if they are being chased. Outside, these rabbits always stay close to a burrow's entrance.

European rabbit mothers give birth inside their burrow. They make soft nests for their babies out of grass and fur. The baby rabbits are born without fur. They are also blind and deaf. They are kept safe and warm inside the burrow. The babies stay inside for the first two weeks of their lives.

FACT!

European rabbits are clever! They can make their burrows on hills. The rain will run down the hill instead of inside their home.

You can see some of the rooms and tunnels inside this warren.

Chapter 4

MEERKATS

FACT FILE

ANIMAL GROUP: Mammal

DIET: Carnivore

HABITATS: Grasslands, plains, and savannas of Africa

FACT!

Meerkats have many entrances to their burrows. They can dig their burrows up to 6.5 feet (2 m) deep.

These meerkats are working together to dig a burrow.

Meerkats live together in burrows. A group of meerkats is called a mob. A mob can have as many as 40 meerkats. Meerkats live in Africa, where it is hot. Sleeping underground in a burrow keeps them cool and safe. Meerkat babies will spend their first three weeks inside the burrow.

Meerkats dig their burrows with their claws. While they are digging, they close their small ears. This keeps the sand and dirt out.

FACT!

Meerkat burrows have different rooms for sleeping and using the bathroom.

This meerkat mother is keeping her babies close.

Outside their burrow, one meerkat will watch for **predators**. It will warn the others to run back inside if there is danger.

Chapter 5

SPADEFOOT TOADS

FACT FILE

ANIMAL GROUP: Amphibian

DIET: Omnivore

HABITATS: Deserts, grasslands, swamps

FACT!

Spadefoot toads sleep inside their burrows curled up in a ball.

This spadefoot toad is resting inside its burrow.

Spadefoot toads get their name from their feet! Part of each back foot looks like a spade, or shovel. These spades are used to dig burrows in sand or dirt. Spadefoot toads dig their burrows facing backward. Their burrows can be deep or closer to the surface. Deeper burrows are dug for colder temperatures.

Spadefoot toads spend most of their time in their burrows. They live alone. They can line part of the burrow with bits of leaves. This makes it cozy. They stay in the burrows during colder months.

The color of this spadefoot toad blends in with the sand outside its burrow.

FACT!

Spadefoot toad burrows can be up to 8 feet (2.4 m) deep. That is about the length of a couch!

These toads come out of their burrows in the late spring or summer. They come out to mate and lay eggs.

MORE ANIMAL BURROWS

NAKED MOLE RAT

Naked mole rats connect their burrows together. These connected burrows can be more than 13,000 feet (3,962 m) long! Naked mole rats use their strong teeth to dig their burrows. Their lips close behind their long teeth. This keeps dirt from getting in their mouths.

PRAIRIE DOGS

Prairie dogs have long toenails for digging burrows. Some burrow in groups called "towns." A town of burrows can have between 30 and 50 entrances. There is a special room near the surface of the burrow. A prairie dog can sit there. It listens for danger before going outside.

CRAYFISH

Some types of crayfish make interesting burrows! They dig small holes in the mud. The mud from each hole piles up. The pile looks like a small volcano or a "mud chimney." Crayfish can create deep burrows with many tunnels and rooms.

GOPHERS

Gophers have strong teeth for digging burrows. They can move rocks and chew through roots. They make tunnels in dirt or snow not far below the ground. Gophers will store their food in rooms farther down. These mammals live alone except for mothers with young babies.

BURROWING BEHAVIOR

There are so many animals that dig burrows! Wombats, puffins, rabbits, meerkats, and spadefoot toads are some of them. Animals hide in burrows to stay safe. Burrows protect baby animals. Burrows also keep animals warm or cool. If you see one, never reach inside! You don't want to scare any animals living there. And you don't want to hurt yourself. You can help keep burrows safe. You can also learn even more about animals that live in burrows!

GLOSSARY

amphibian (am-FIB-ee-uhn) a cold-blooded animal with a backbone that lives in water and breathes with gills when young; as an adult, it develops lungs and lives on land

burrow (BUR-oh) a tunnel or hole in the ground made or used as a home by an animal

carnivore (KAHR-nuh-vor) an animal that eats meat

habitat (HAB-i-tat) the place where an animal or a plant is usually found

herbivore (HUR-buh-vor) an animal that only eats plants

mammal (MAM-uhl) a warm-blooded animal that has fur and usually gives birth to live babies

marsupial (mahr-SOO-pee-uhl) any of a large group of animals that includes the kangaroo, the koala, and the opossum; female marsupials carry their babies in pouches

mate to join together to produce babies

omnivore (AHM-nuh-vor) an animal that eats both plants and meat

predator (PRED-uh-tur) an animal that lives by hunting other animals for food

spade (spayd) a tool used for digging, with a long, sturdy handle and a flat blade that you can push into the earth with your foot

INDEX

Page numbers in **bold** indicate images.

ABOUT THE AUTHOR

Claire Caprioli loves learning and writing about animals! Gophers and moles make burrows in her backyard. You can learn more about her by visiting clairecaprioli.com.